GAS

© Aladdin Books Ltd

Designed and produced by
Aladdin Books Ltd
70 Old Compton St
London W1

First published in the
United States 1985 by
Gloucester Press
387 Park Avenue South
New York, 10016

ISBN 0531 034879

Printed in Belgium

Photographic credits:
Cover and pages 18 and 19, Frank Spooner;
pages 8 and 10, Zefa; pages 13, 14 and 16,
Daily Telegraph Colour Library; pages 20, 22
and 23, GEC; page 25, ICI Agricultural
Division UK; page 26, Peter Fraenkel.

The cover picture shows gas being flared at
night in the North Sea.

GUY ARNOLD

Illustrated by
Ron Hayward Associates

Consultant
Stuart Boyle

Gloucester Press
New York : Toronto

Introduction

It is easy to forget how important energy is to us all. We need it for heating and lighting our houses, schools and offices and for fuel.

The energy crisis of recent years has meant that gas has become more and more important as a source of power. Scientists constantly search for new reserves and the wasteful practice of "flaring," burning off the gas which is found with oil, has been cut back. This book describes ways of getting power from this valuable source of energy.

Flaring, or burning, gas in an oilfield

Contents

Energy from gas

Have you ever seen blue flames on top of a kitchen stove and wondered where they come from? These flames are caused by the burning of gas. Gas is one of our cleanest energy sources. It is also easy to transport and store.

The world has gas because for millions of years much of the Earth was covered by sea. When the plants and animals which lived in this sea died, their remains settled on the seabed and decayed. These remains have given us the "vapor" we call gas.

Giant gas storage tanks

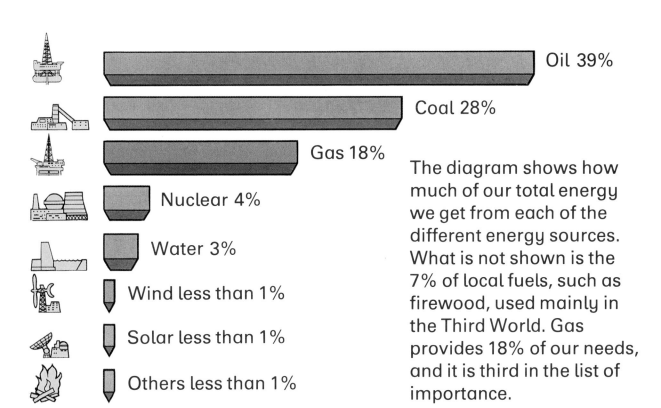

Oil 39%

Coal 28%

Gas 18%

Nuclear 4%

Water 3%

Wind less than 1%

Solar less than 1%

Others less than 1%

The diagram shows how much of our total energy we get from each of the different energy sources. What is not shown is the 7% of local fuels, such as firewood, used mainly in the Third World. Gas provides 18% of our needs, and it is third in the list of importance.

Finding gas

In the past we got most of our gas by heating coal. Today, most of the gas used is "natural" gas, found deep below the land or seabed.

Scientists have ways of searching beneath the Earth's surface for gas. First they set off explosions which send soundwaves into the ground. From the echoes which come back, they can tell where the gas "fields" are.

A deep hole is then dug underground by an "exploration" rig. This consists of a "derrick," a tower like an electricity pylon, and a long drill with a "bit" on the end. The photograph shows the bit plunging into the sea to the gas below.

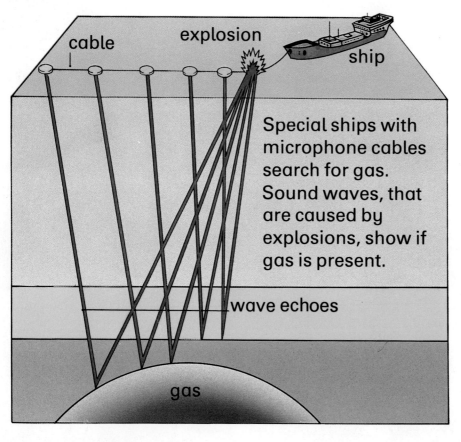

cable   explosion   ship

Special ships with microphone cables search for gas. Sound waves, that are caused by explosions, show if gas is present.

wave echoes

gas

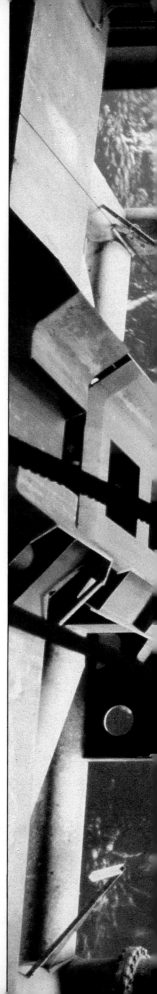

Gas platforms

If gas is found on land, wells are drilled and the gas rises naturally to the surface.
But if the gas is found at sea, getting it out is more complicated. Giant production platforms have to be towed out to where the rigs have found gas, and put in position.

A semisubmersible rig is used for deep-water exploration.

An offshore production platform is both a factory and hotel, with the workforce on site for two weeks at a time. The jobs are tough and have to be carried out even when the platform is buffeted by rain, snow and gales.

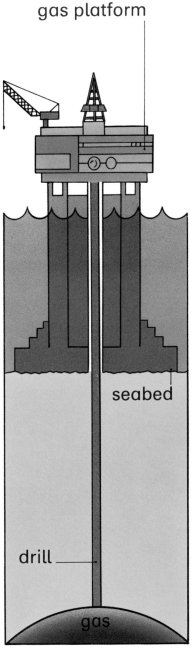

gas platform

seabed

drill

gas

Production platforms are huge structures that sit on the seabed. They work 24 hours a day, gathering up the flow of gas from the rocks far below.

Piping gas

The natural gas which comes ashore is really a mixture of gases and chemicals. These have to be separated out before we can get "methane" – the gas which burns best. Then it is carried by tanker or pipeline to its final destination.

There are so many gas pipelines in the world that a map of them would look like a road map! A new one is being built, to take gas 4,400km (2,734 miles) from Siberia to France.

Gas is cleaned and separated in these pipes

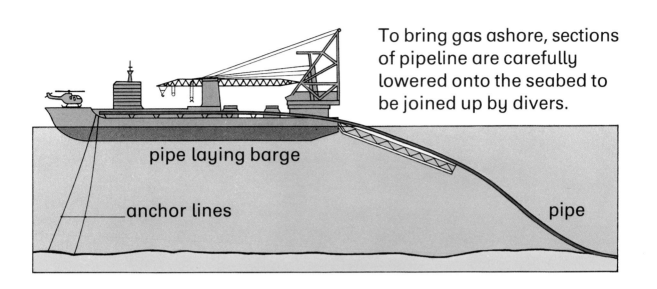

To bring gas ashore, sections of pipeline are carefully lowered onto the seabed to be joined up by divers.

pipe laying barge

anchor lines

pipe

Liquid gas

Gas comes out of the ground as a vapor. When it is cooled, or "refrigerated," it changes into liquid. This reduces its "volume," and makes it easy to move.

There are two kinds of liquid gas. There is Liquid Natural Gas (LNG) and Liquid Petroleum Gas (LPG). Both are moved by pipeline or shipped across the sea in huge tankers. For safety reasons, these ships have to conform to strict international rules. LPG is also carried by road to places where there are no gas pipelines.

Liquid gas being shipped from Algeria

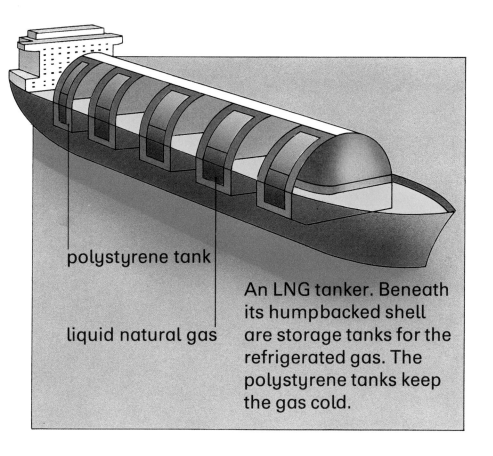

polystyrene tank

liquid natural gas

An LNG tanker. Beneath its humpbacked shell are storage tanks for the refrigerated gas. The polystyrene tanks keep the gas cold.

METHANE PROGRESS

Mobile power station

The mobile power station on the road . . .

. . . and in action

Many power stations work by burning gas.
The heat from the flames is used to make, or
"generate" electricity. In fact, gas itself is
often a cheaper form of energy than electricity.
Electricity usually has to be made by burning
some other material like gas, coal or oil.

Gas is also used to provide energy for new
"mobile" power stations. These are small
power stations which are moved by road or
railroad to places that have no electricity, or to
areas where extra supplies are needed.

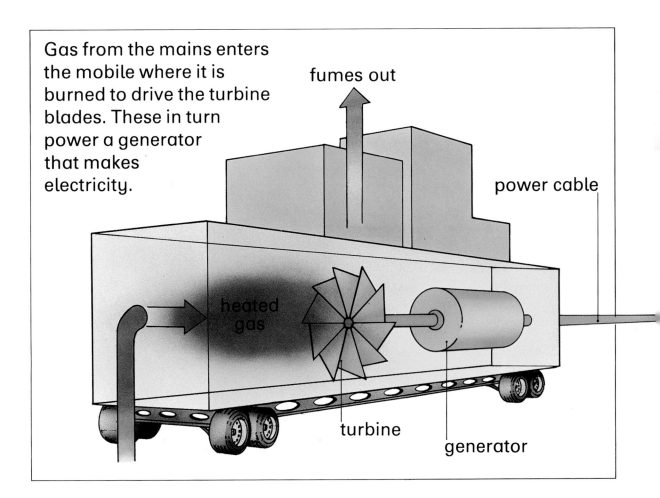

Gas from the mains enters
the mobile where it is
burned to drive the turbine
blades. These in turn
power a generator
that makes
electricity.

fumes out

power cable

heated gas

turbine

generator

Gas in industry

Gas is not only used in power stations to make electricity, it is also burned in factories. It is cleaner to burn than coal. It comes into the factory in pipes and does not have to be stored in piles like coal. Many furnaces are powered by gas, and some steelworks use it to smelt ore in blast furnaces.

These big engines are driven by natural gas

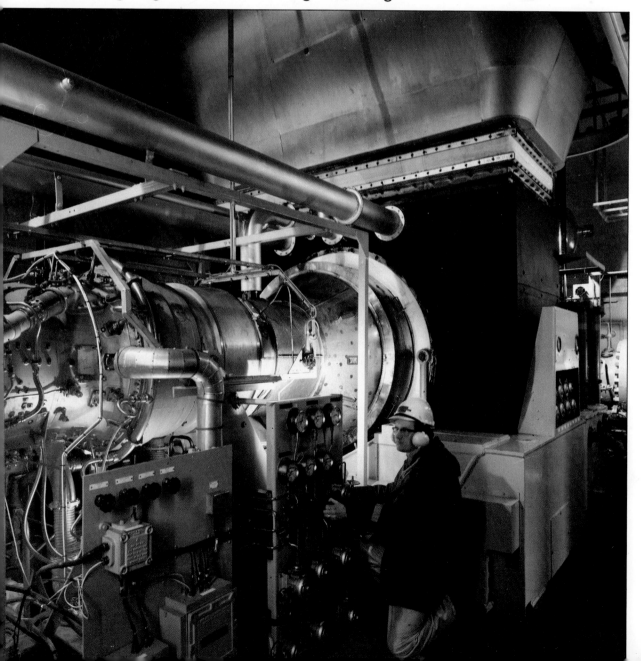

Gas is also used in welding, and to drive huge engines. Fierce jets of gas make the intense flames that are needed. Did you know that china mugs, plates, cups and saucers are made hard by "firing" them in a gas furnace? Gas is also used in the production of glass. A jet of gas softens the glass so that it can be shaped.

Molding glass ornaments with a gas jet

Many uses of gas

Many of us have gas appliances in our homes: stoves, heaters, hot water boilers and heating systems.

But gas is more than a source of energy. Many other things are derived from it. Fibers in clothes, plastic equipment of all sorts; even the stuffing in cushions may come from gas.

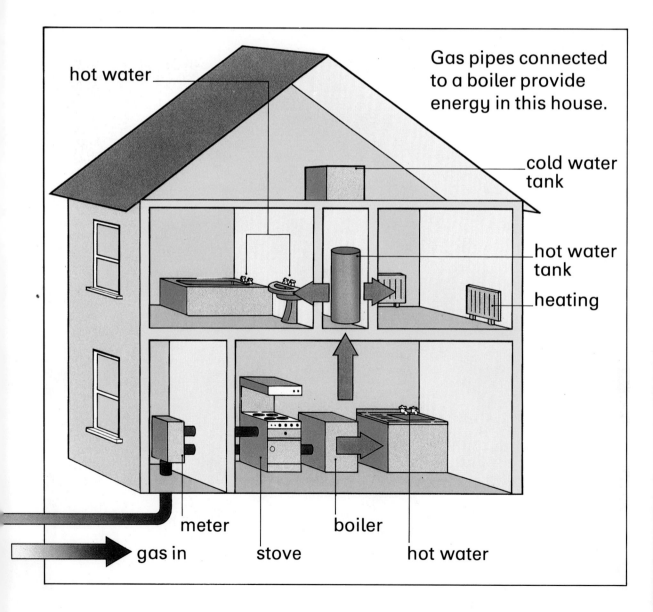

hot water

Gas pipes connected to a boiler provide energy in this house.

cold water tank

hot water tank

heating

meter

gas in

stove

boiler

hot water

Gas is also used to help make special food for animals! This food is called "pruteen," and is used to feed pigs, poultry and fish.

Fertilizers, which farmers sprinkle on their land, is often made by using gas. These fertilizers make the land rich, and help the farmers grow more food.

Pigs eating pruteen feedstock

This Chinese tractor runs on biogas

Making biogas

Many countries in the world do not have reserves of gas, and they cannot afford to buy gas from other countries. So some of the poorer countries now make their own.

If you go to China you will see people collecting animal and human waste every day. This waste is put into sealed containers and quickly changes into a liquid.

Soon this liquid gives off a type of gas called "biogas." It is used in farms and factories, and in homes for cooking and heating. Many people in the world now get their gas in this way.

pig

chicken

A special tank changes the manure of pigs, hens and other farm animals into biogas. Biogas is really methane.

methane out

methane storage tank

manure in

manure conversion tank

The future of gas

The search for gas goes on all the time. In the future, new ways of producing and using it may be invented. In fact, we now have the natural gas "fuel cell" which can produce electricity from gas without any flames. Small fuel cells may soon be used in houses and cars.

But gas can be dangerous, and great care must be taken in connecting gas pipes to buildings to avoid accidental explosions. At the same time, it is a good friend. It is a clean, efficient form of energy which we must not waste.

A gas pipeline on fire in the USSR

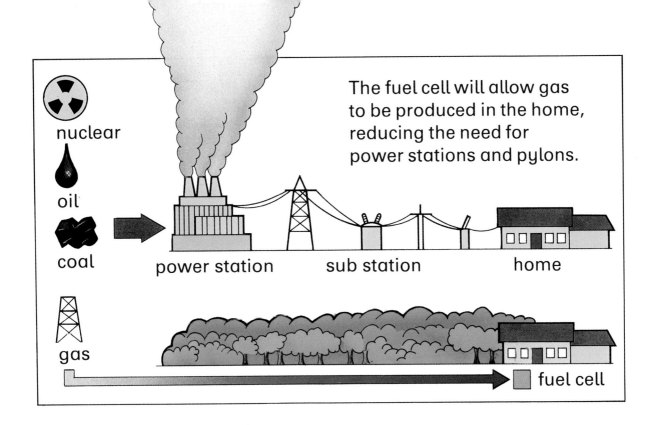

nuclear

oil

coal

gas

The fuel cell will allow gas to be produced in the home, reducing the need for power stations and pylons.

power station   sub station   home

fuel cell

Fact file 1

When gas is found with oil it is called "associated" gas. Gas is lighter than oil, so it rises above it when both are trapped under non-porous rock. Sometimes it is found with water too.

Deposits of gas may be found without oil or water. Movements in the Earth's crust, or "rock faults," may cause this. They have shifted the gas away from its original spot.

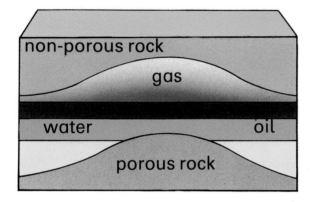

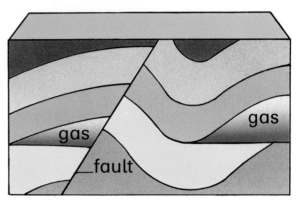

Drilling rigs are used for gas exploration. The jack-up rig is for shallow water. The floating semisubmersible is for deeper water. In very deep water, drill ships are used.

Production platforms are put in place when gas production goes ahead. They are so expensive to build that one platform has to drain gas from as many as 24 wells.

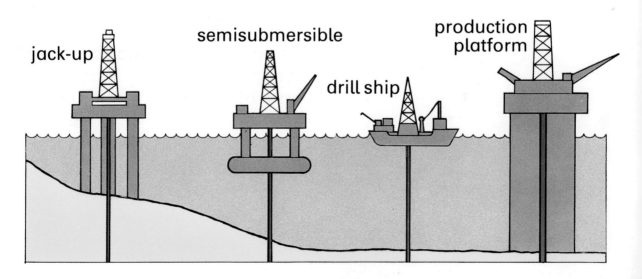

doctor   deckhand   chef   diver   engineer   helicopter pilot

The drawing below shows how flexible "drill strings" connect the platform to the gas field. These are built up, section by section, from the platform, and can be as long as 2 km (1.25 miles).

Production platforms and rigs need many people to run them. Many specialized jobs have to be done. Because of the tough conditions the crew must be well trained and very fit.

Life on a production platform or exploration rig is not easy. Crew members are away from home for two weeks at a time. There are few leisure activities apart from watching movies and eating! Alcohol is forbidden. Because of the fire risks, cigarette smoking is restricted to certain areas.

An exploration rig may be at sea for up to 90 days. It will have a crew of 75, and will need 3,050 tonnes (3,362 tons) of supplies. Two supply ships service the rig. There is always a helicopter link with shore. Rigs keep close radio contact with a land base. In an emergency any casualties are flown to the hospital on shore.

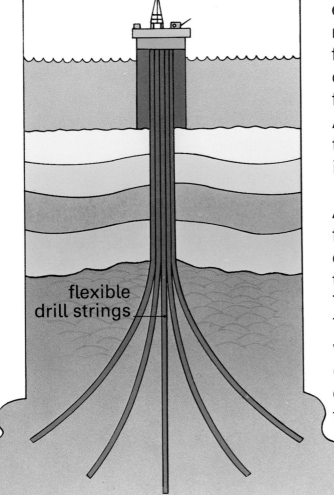

flexible drill strings

Fact file 2

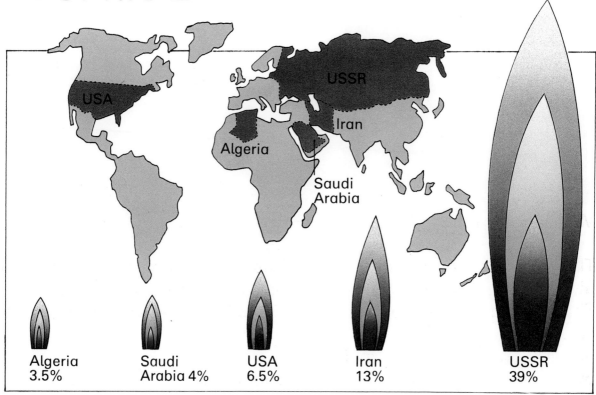

World gas producers

Discoveries of gas are made every year. Its importance as a form of energy is always growing. Estimates show that the world has 88,054 trillion cubic meters (3,109,715 trillion cubic feet) in reserve.

Forty percent of the world's natural gas is in the USSR. A great deal is sold abroad.

Demand for gas is highest in the USA. It has 6.5% of the world's supplies, but imports more from neighboring Mexico and Canada.

Politics has played its part in Iran's use of gas. It has 13% of the world's supplies. In recent years it has not been a major exporter. It wants to keep its supplies.

Huge reserves of gas and oil are in Saudi Arabia. A scheme for gathering this gas will add 10% to the world's supplies.

Algeria in North Africa has the fifth largest gas fields. Located under the Sahara Desert, the Trans-Mediterranean pipeline carries this gas to Europe.

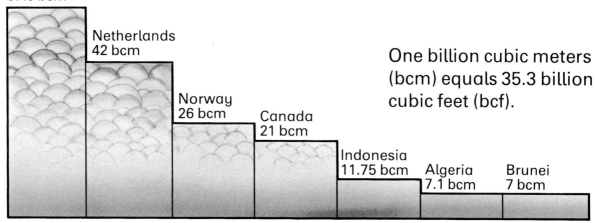

USSR
57.5 bcm

Netherlands
42 bcm

Norway
26 bcm

Canada
21 bcm

Indonesia
11.75 bcm

Algeria
7.1 bcm

Brunei
7 bcm

One billion cubic meters (bcm) equals 35.3 billion cubic feet (bcf).

Major world gas exporters

The main gas producers are not always the major exporters. This depends on the producing countrys' own needs. Some actually buy gas to make their own reserves last longer.

In 1982 the leading producers were: USSR 501 billion cubic meters; USA 497 bcm; Canada 70 bcm; Netherlands 68 bcm; Romania 39 bcm; UK 38 bcm.

Iran's gas reserves are twice as high as those of the USA. The USSR is keen to buy some of this gas.

Japan's demand for gas is growing. It imports most of the world's traded LNG.

Australia is developing its huge gas resources. About half will eventually go to Japan.

378 cubic meters
(13,350 cubic feet)
per year

1.9 bcm
(67 billion cubic feet) per year

A gas stove uses, on average, 378 cubic meters (13,350 cubic feet) of gas a year. This is very little when compared to the amount a factory uses.

An average size factory – one producing fruit juice, for example – will use six and a half million times as much gas a year as a kitchen stove.

Glossary

Biogas A gas made from organic life or human or animal waste material.

Bit The cutting or boring end of a drill.

Fertilizer A form of artificial manure made from chemical products.

Jack-up A term for a rig that can be raised to different heights from the seabed by extending its legs.

Liquid Natural Gas (LNG) A gas that has been cooled (refrigerated) until it becomes a liquid that is easier to transport and store.

Liquid Petroleum Gas (LPG) A gas made from petroleum products and then cooled (refrigerated) until it becomes a liquid.

Refrigerated Exposed to extreme cold to freeze and preserve until needed.

Semisubmersible A rig that "floats" at sea; giant ballast tanks hold it in place.

Terminals Storage areas where gas is kept before distribution by pipeline or tanker.

Index

Acknowledgements
The publishers wish to thank the following
organisations who have helped in the
preparation of this book:
British Petroleum Co., British Gas
Corporation, B.P. Chemicals, Central
Electricity Generating Board UK, Friends of
the Earth, ICI Agricultural Division UK, Shell
International Petroleum Co. Ltd., UK
Department of Energy, World Gas Magazine.

PRINTED IN BELGIUM BY

INTERNATIONAL BOOK PRODUCTION

J   87-1342
665.7
ARN   Arnold

Gas.

JAN   2   B 1 3 6 1 1
FEB   B 1 2 6 9 2
FEB   B 1 3 5 7 1
MAR   7   B 1 3 5 7 1
NOV   8   B 1 7 2 0 8

DEC 30   B 1 3 5 7 1
MAR 24   B 1 3 5 7 1
AUG   3   B 1 7 6 6 3

Free Public Library
Bridgeton, New Jersey

———

Most books are issued for two weeks, and are subject to renewal for two additional weeks.

Five cents a day is charged for all books kept over time.

The borrower is responsible for books charged to his name.